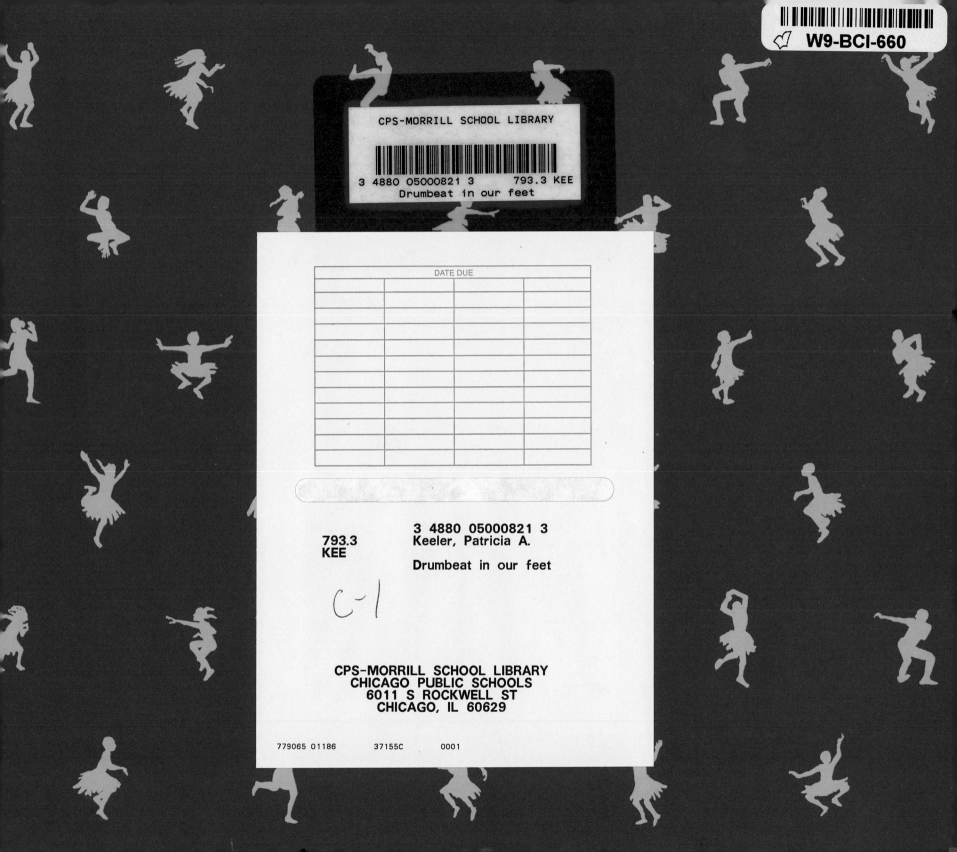

DrumBeat in Our Feet

by Patricia A. Keeler and Júlio T. Leitão

illustrated by Patricia A. Keeler

Lee & Low Books Inc. · New York

Text copyright © 2006 by Patricia A. Keeler and Júlio T. Leitão
Illustrations copyright © 2006 by Patricia A. Keeler

LEE & LOW BOOKS Inc., 95 Madison Avenue, New York, NY 10016 leeandlow.com

Manufactured in China

Book design by Tania Garcia
Book production by The Kids at Our House

The text is set in Skia
The illustrations are rendered in watercolor and colored pencil

All photos by Patricia A. Keeler used with permission

10 9 8 7 6 5 4 3 2 1
First Edition

Library of Congress Cataloging-in-Publication Data
Keeler, Patricia A.
Drumbeat in our feet / by Patricia A. Keeler and Júlio T. Leitão ; illustrated by Patricia A. Keeler.
p. cm.
Summary: "Informative passages and lyrical verse explore the history and rhythmic qualities of traditional
African dance as performed long ago and today. Note about Harlem-based African dance troupe Batoto Yetu,
photographs, and map in backmatter"—Provided by publisher.
ISBN-13: 978-1-58430-264-3   ISBN-10: 1-58430-264-X
1. Dance—Africa—Juvenile literature. 2. Dance, Black—Juvenile literature. I. Leitão, Júlio. II. Title.
GV1705.K44 2006
793.3'196—dc22   2005031072

Many thanks to the talented and hardworking children, parents, and grandparents who make up the Batoto Yetu family. The children's stories and their beautiful, powerful dancing inspired the creation of this book
— P.A.K. and J.T.L.

For Ida, mukalenga — P.A.K.

To my beloved wife, Kenza; my daughter, Luena; and my friend David Kapuadi for his guidance and support
— J.T.L.

Origins of African Dance

There's an old African saying, "If you can walk, you can dance. If you can talk, you can sing." Music, song, and dance are vital parts of daily life in Africa, and have been for as far back as anyone can remember.

The history of African music and dance is as rich and diverse as the land itself. Of the more than fifty countries in Africa today, there are tiny countries such as Togo and large countries such as the Democratic Republic of the Congo. Some countries border an ocean. Some are blanketed with grasslands called savannas. Others are mostly desert, and still others are crowned with dense forests.

Ethnically diverse groups of people live across this varied landscape—from the tall Masai of Tanzania to the small Mbuti of the Democratic Republic of the Congo. Each group has its own special dance steps and music, reflecting that particular land and culture. Together these unique forms of expression create the vibrant tapestry that is African dance.

Coming from Brooklyn, coming from Harlem,
The Bronx and down the subway lines.

We're African dancers, telling our stories,
The way they did a long time ago.

Passing the Traditions

Dances have been passed down from generation to generation for thousands of years, carrying the past into the present. The dances tell stories and share history and myths from long, long ago.

Today as in the past, learning about culture and traditions is an important part of being African. Grandparents, parents, and children know the dances, songs, and stories that are part of their community.

Traditional dances are kept alive by passing them on to younger generations. Most African children learn the steps by watching and imitating dancers at celebrations. They also learn from relatives, friends, and other members of their communities.

Sambai is our teacher,
Sambai from Angola,
Sambai from—
The Luba tribe.

Teaching us the songs,
Teaching us the dances,
Like his mamu taught him
When he was just a boy.

Types of Dances

Each community has dances for different occasions. There are dances for weddings and funerals, for naming children, and moving to a new home. There are celebration dances and healing dances. Dances mark changes in the seasons—celebrating the arrival of the rainy season and the first fruit of the harvest. Others caution children about what might happen if they don't listen to their elders.

There are also dances about growing up, or coming-of-age. These dances play an important part in rituals performed when boys and girls become adults. In central Africa coming-of-age rituals for boys are called the *Mukanda*. Boys leave their village to compete in tests of strength and endurance and participate in Mukanda dances. They return to their village as men.

Fearless boys
Dancing
the Mukanda
Leaping
and spinning,
Shouting out—
Mukanda
Prá-ká-tá!

IMAGE DANCES

Dances that mimic animal movements are sometimes called *image dances*. These age-old dance steps were developed by people who watched the animals around them—antelopes bounding across the savannas, elephants lumbering to water holes, snakes slithering through the mud under low-flying birds.

The people noticed that some animals moved swiftly, while others moved with heavy steps. Some animals were agile; others awkward. Africans created dances to reflect these qualities.

Arms spread like bird wings, backbones curved like snakes,
we sprint away like antelopes do. Eh-way! Eh-way! Eh-way!

Costumes and Body Painting

Throughout Africa dancers generally perform in colorful costumes. It is common for female dancers to wear blouses and head wraps, and both men and women wear dried-grass skirts.

In spite of some similarities, costumes vary widely. On the west coast, the Samo of Burkina Faso wear costumes covered in cowrie shells from the sea. In the Democratic Republic of the Congo, the Mbuti, a forest people, wear leaf skirts. And the Salampasu, known for their hunting skills, wear leopard skins.

In addition some dancers paint their faces and bodies with colorful designs. The Yoruba of Nigeria paint spirals, triangles, and diagonal lines. Some of their body painting resembles drums or snakes. Among the Shona of Zimbabwe, the color red establishes contact with the spirits; and for the Bamum men of Cameroon, black or blue face paint shows fierceness.

Getting ready for the show.
Painting our bodies.
Lines on our faces,
Diamonds on our arms.
And butterflies—
in our bellies!

SPIRITS AND ANCESTORS

Many Africans believe in spirits with special powers. Spirits are ancestors, family members who have passed away, who guide and protect people in the living world. People can ask their ancestral spirits for help in making crops grow, curing illness, and even guiding their dance steps.

At the entrance to some villages in southwest and central Africa there are two statues—one of a man and one of a woman. When a man dies and passes to the next world, the villagers paint a white dot on the statue of the man. When a woman in the village passes, a white dot is painted on the statue of the woman.

This way of honoring spirits is also used by some dancers, such as those from the Democratic Republic of the Congo. The dancers paint white dots, each representing an ancestor, on their bodies before performing.

Thinking about the ancestors
Once young like us—

Dancing on
African soil

Dancing under
African clouds

Dancing in
African rain

Breathing in
African air

LIBATIONS

When a group of people sits down for a meal, sooner or later a cup will tip and a drink will spill. There is an African belief that the spill occurs because the ancestors have joined the gathering.

Before a performance some dancers pour a small puddle of water on the floor. This ceremony is called *libations*, and the water—like a spilled drink—symbolizes the ancestors joining the celebration.

One by one the dancers step into the puddle. This connects the dancers with the ancestors as they ask the ancestors to guide their performance.

Making a circle, Mayi means water, water means life.

MUSICAL INSTRUMENTS

All across Africa dancers perform to the rhythmic sounds of drums, rattles, and xylophones.

The most popular instrument in Africa is the drum. Drums pound out the rhythms of the dances. They are the heartbeat of African song and dance. A traditional drum is carved from a single tree trunk, and the top is covered with goatskin.

Rattles are made from gourds that grow on vines along the ground. When the gourds are dried and shaken, the seeds inside rattle.

Xylophones are made of a row of wooden bars. Each bar is a different length. When a bar is struck, a hollow gourd underneath amplifies the sound.

Time for the show!
Drums rumble!
Drums thunder!
Rattles shake and chatter.
Hear the sound of the xylophone chime.

Feel the rhythm,
African rhythm!
Feel the drumbeat,
African beat!

DRUMS AND DRUMBEAT SIGNALS

There are many types of drums in Africa. In central Africa narrow, conical *Ngoma* drums are tied to the drummer above the waist and held between the knees. Message drums, made from hollowed-out logs, sit horizontally on the ground. The beat of the message drum can be heard for miles.

Talking drums of western Africa are hourglass shaped. Cords are strung back and forth from the skins fastened over each end. Placing the drum under one arm, a drummer squeezes the cords, making the drum skins tighter and changing the pitch of the drumbeat.

Drumbeats set the rhythm for the dance, and they also tell the dancers what to do. Drummers teach the dancers a special riff, a pattern of drumbeats. The riff is called a *drum break*. When dancers hear the drum break, it signals them to start dancing, change steps, or stop.

Listen up! The drums are talking!
Listen for the drum break.
Hear the beat: Doom, doom, da!
Tet da-da dum, Tet da-da dum, Doom, doom, da!
Hear the drum break? Dance, dance, dance!

Call-and-Response

In some villages dancers line up, one behind the other, and process, or dance, their way to the place where a celebration or ritual will take place. This may be the center of a village, a river, a field, or a burial ground. As they go, one of the dancers begins a call-and-response song. The leader calls out lines of a song, and those around him give the refrain.

This ancient form of song is enjoyed all over Africa. Call-and-response helps focus the attention of the dancers. It also invites other villagers and ancestral spirits to join the excitement of the celebration.

Basunhi dikumi. (Ten of us always go to get water.)

Mayi! (Water!)

Fika ku ditua. (We arrive at the river.)

Mayi! (Water!)

Ku sangana keema! (We find monkeys!)

MASKED DANCERS

Masked dancers are the most sacred dancers in Africa. They wear costumes that cover them from head to toe, including masks symbolizing spirits of animals or people. Traditionally, no one knows who the dancers are. When they are in costume they become living forms of the spirits represented by the masks.

Masked dancers bring the spirits closer to the living world. They are thought to balance good and bad energy and to keep nature in harmony. Their dances can cleanse fields so that crops will grow or rain will fall.

Yoruba masks for motherhood,
Big mamas of angelic forces, big mamas of abundance.
Hips are swaying, whirling 'round, making a good wind blow!

DANCE PERFORMANCE

Today in Africa dance troupes sometimes perform in theaters. But theaters tend to separate dancers from the audience, so many dancers prefer to perform the old way—in the center of a village lit by a campfire and surrounded by their audience.

Traditional dance celebrations are contagious! The sound of the drums travels through the forests and across the savannas. Soon neighboring villagers arrive to join in the festivities. Some dance celebrations start at dawn and go on until dark. Others go on for days.

At times the whole audience is clapping, singing, and dancing. Performers and spectators, grandparents, parents, and children all dance together as one.

Flowing like water   Rhythms going faster

Drums pounding louder

Like our heartbeats

We are the children of the ancestors, singing the songs, dancing the steps to a

story that never ends. African rhythm in our steps. African drumbeat in our feet!

Batoto Yetu
A New Generation of African Dancers

The theater darkens. A pulsating beat thunders through the audience. Then, as if by magic, the Batoto Yetu dancers appear in the aisles and make their way onto the stage. With painted faces and swirling grass skirts, the dancers leap and spin. They swivel their hips and thrust their hands toward the ceiling. They sing in Tshiluba, an African language. Members of the sold-out crowd at Carnegie Hall in New York City clap their hands and stomp their feet!

The Harlem, New York-based African dance troupe Batoto Yetu has performed in the United States, South America, Canada, Europe, and Africa. The dancers have delighted passers-by on city playgrounds and celebrities at the Apollo Theater. They have fascinated children watching *Sesame Street* at home and dignitaries at the United Nations.

Batoto Yetu was brought to life in 1990 by Angolan dancer and choreographer Júlio Leitão. While teaching African dance to adults at the National Black Theater, Júlio noticed bright-eyed, curious children watching from off stage. He saw that they couldn't stop moving their feet to the rhythm of the drums. One week later on a Harlem playground, Júlio started Batoto Yetu with just seven children.

Batoto Yetu means "our children" in Swahili. Since the group began, more than two thousand children ages four to seventeen have participated. Not only do they learn dance steps, they also learn the importance of tradition, dedication, and teamwork.

As the dancers reach their late teens, college and jobs draw them away from the troupe. Júlio dedicates each dancer's last performance to the boy or girl who is leaving, but Batoto Yetu graduates are always welcome to come back and perform. Working with Batoto Yetu gives Júlio the chance to live the childhood that was taken from him. In 1975 when Júlio was a young boy, he and most of his family fled from the civil war in Angola. They eventually made their way to Portugal, where for a time they lived in an abandoned jail.

"Whenever we went to sleep my mother sang," Júlio recalls. "That's the way you survive when you don't have a home. Your dreams, and the music and dance, keep you going." Batoto Yetu dancers, musicians, and parent volunteers gather most Saturdays at a public school auditorium. The dancers work hard. They learn to breathe and warm up properly. They are taught to focus and dance from the inside out. When it is time for the practice to begin, the musical director, Rodderick Jackson, begins a drumbeat, and Júlio calls, "Let's dance!" There are no mirrors in the room. The dancers move to what they feel, not by how they look. The joy the children experience is obvious to all who watch them. "Once you learn how to do African dance," says one young dancer, "you'll never stop dancing!"

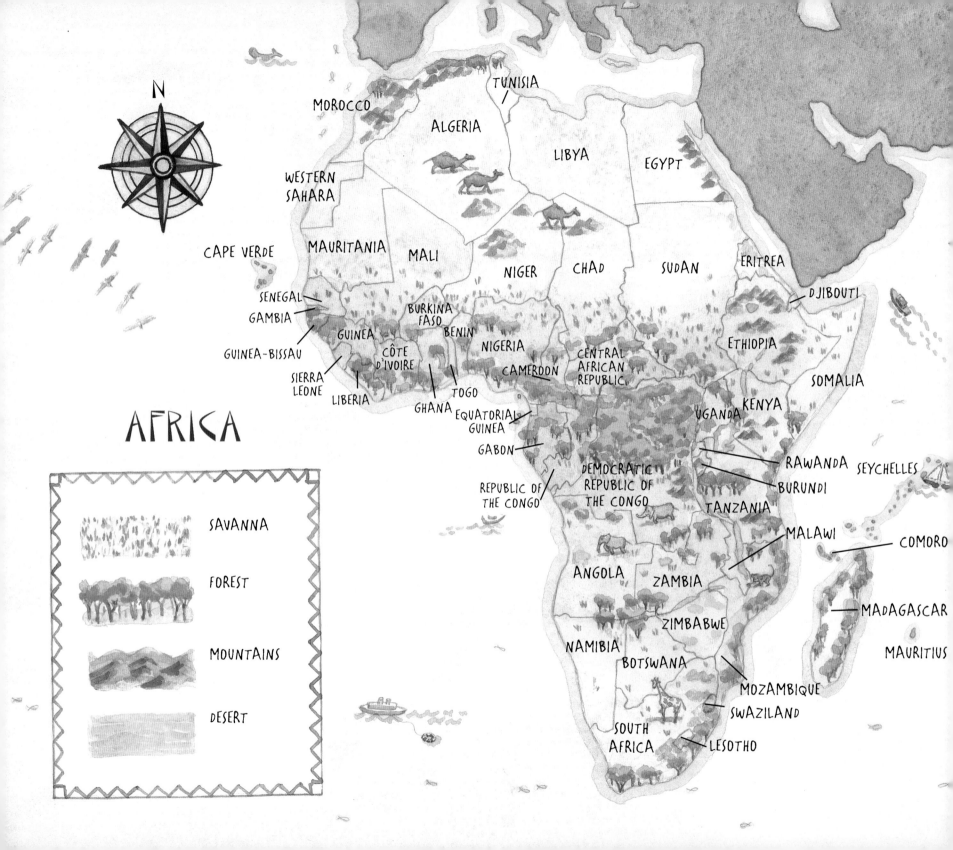

Pronunciation Guide

Many of the African words in this book have been adapted into English from native languages. Some variations in spelling and pronunciation may exist.

Angola (ang-GO-lah)
Bamum (BA-moom)
Basunhi dikumi (ba-SU-nee DEE-koom-ee)
Batoto Yetu (BA-toe-toe yeh-TOO)
Burkina Faso (bur-KEY-na FA-so)
Cameroon (kam-a-ROON)
Congo (KON-go)
Fika ku ditua (fee-KA KOO dee-TOO-uh)
Ku sangana kima (KOO san-YAN-ah kee-MA)
libations (lie-BAY-shunz)
Luba (LOO-bah)
Masai (ma-SIGH)

mayi (MY-ee)
Mbuti (em-BOO-tee)
Mukanda (moo-KAN-dah)
Ngoma (en-GO-ma)
Nigeria (nigh-JEER-ee-uh)
Salampasu (sa-LAM-pa-su)
Samo (sa-MU)
Sawadugu (sa-WA-doo-goo)
Shona (sho-NA)
Togo (TOE-go)
Yoruba (YOUR-a-ba *or* YO-roo-ba)
Zimbabwe (zim-BOB-we *or* zim-BOB-way)

Author's Sources

Huet, Michel. *The Dance, Art and Ritual of Africa.* New York: Pantheon Books, 1978.

———, and Claude Savary. *Africa Dances.* London: Thames and Hudson Ltd, 1995.

Welsh-Asante, Kariamu. *African Dance.* New York: Chelsea House Publishers, 2004.

———. *African Dance: An Artistic, Historical and Philosophical Inquiry.* Lawrenceville, New Jersey: Africa World Press, Inc, 1997.

———. *Zimbabwe Dance: Rhythmic Forces, Ancestral Voices—An Aesthetic Analysis.* Lawrenceville, New Jersey: Africa World Press, Inc., 1997.